This book is dedicated to my wife. Withou[t]
throughout my journey, none of this

The information contained in this guide is for informational purposes only.

All advice given is based on my opinion and experience. Any amount of earnings and success disclosed in this guide shouldn't be considered average.

The material in this guide may include information, products or services by third parties. Third-party materials comprise of the products and opinions expressed by their owners. I don't assume responsibility or liability for any third-party material or opinions.

The potential use of these recommended third-party materials doesn't guarantee any success and/or earnings related to your sportswriting career. Publication of this material is simply recommendations based on what worked best for me to attain my goal.

No part of this book shall be reproduced, transmitted or sold in whole or in part in any form, without the prior written consent of the author.

Users of this guide are advised to do their own due diligence when it comes to making decisions for their respective sportswriting careers. All information, products and services provided should also be verified with your own research.

By reading this, you agree I'm not responsible for the success or failure of your business decisions, relating to any information presented in this guide.

Prologue

Throughout childhood and even into adulthood, my mornings were never complete without watching at least one episode of Sportscenter. From the moment I can remember anything, sports have been a huge part of my personality.

As a kid, the two sports I played competitively were basketball and baseball. Since I peaked as a basketball player in fifth grade, my time in baseball was much more extensive and successful.

Following a four-year career in high school, I went on to play Club Baseball at Sacred Heart University. While studying Sport Management, I was fortunate enough to capture league MVP honors in my senior season.

Before settling down in the "real world," my baseball career took me to Joliet, Illinois for a professional tryout. Since there isn't a big market for 5'8" first basemen who are table setters and not power hitters, that's where my time as a player ended. I couldn't have predicted what was ahead, though.

Given how tough the job market was when I graduated (in 2009), my first full-time job wasn't in sports. Still wanting to stay involved on some level, I knew there had to be a way to make an impact.

When I began my sports blogging career in August 2011, I had no idea what to do or how to accomplish it. Although I never took a journalism or communications class beyond the introductory level, starting a baseball blog (called On The Way Home) as a hobby was a great way to stay connected to the game I loved, while also keeping me out of trouble.

Unexpectedly, this hobby quickly turned into an intense passion, then transformed into a legitimate career.

Since my first post for On the Way Home, I've published over 2,000 articles and generated nearly 10 million page views. My writing career has taken many twists and turns, but I've enjoyed some fantastic opportunities in the process.

I wanted to write this book for those with a desire to break into the sports journalism world but don't know where to start. However, the information outlined in the following pages isn't a "system" that will propel you somewhere overnight.

It's a collection of all my experiences and what I think is most important, along with resources I found most helpful, so you don't have to experience the same amount of trial and error I did.

When reading a lot of other "how to" books and articles, the beginning is overlooked an awful lot, especially since it's typically the hardest part. There's a lack of actionable steps to get people going in the right direction and gain some momentum.

That's my goal here—to show you what worked and what didn't work for me, while also providing concrete options to experiment with as you start building a solid and engaging audience.

As a thank-you for checking this book out, I want to provide some special resources, too!

The contents of this book have been turned into an online course at Udemy. Retail price is $19.99, but all Sports Blogging 101 readers can use the SPORTSBLOGGING8 coupon code to access a 50% discount. I'd also love it if you joined my email newsletter by signing up at tinyletter.com/musicom.

Finally, once you're done reading and absorbing all this information, I'm happy to offer a free 30-minute consultation in order to help you get started. When the time comes, send me an email at matt.musico8@gmail.com.

Table of Contents

Intro: Why do you want to be a sportswriter?

Chapter 1: What should you write about?

Chapter 2: The importance of a content strategy

Chapter 3: Establishing a social media presence

Chapter 4: Taking your blog to the next level

Chapter 5: Taking your credibility to the next level

Chapter 6: Turning your passion into profit

INTRODUCTION:

Why do you want to write about sports?

The sports industry generates billions of dollars annually between ticket sales, licensed merchandise, TV deals, and much more.

There is a ton of demand for the product being created. Thanks to modern day technology, fans are consuming news, rumors, and all kinds of content via countless digital platforms 24 hours a day, seven days a week.

Are you one of those people that can never get enough with regard to your favorite team(s) and/or sport(s)?

Do you have an overwhelming feeling to share your opinion?

Are your comments nearly as long as the articles you read?

Have you always wanted to start your own sports blog, but thought it was too late because you didn't study communications or journalism in college?

Better yet, do you want to have experience by the time you get to college?

It takes time and effort to become a successful sportswriter, and it's a humbling profession. Although the market appears saturated because there are so many websites out there, now is the best time to dive in.

Since no two people are exactly alike, no two writing styles and opinions are exactly alike, either. What you have to share with potential readers is special and unique. Nobody else can create the kind of content you can create.

Getting started—especially without having any kind of formal education or direction—can be daunting. That's exactly why I wrote this book. Not long ago, I was in the same spot you're sitting in right now, wondering if I could make sportswriting a career and how to go about doing that.

This won't happen overnight. Getting established and becoming credible to millions of readers hungry for original and unique content is a process.

Despite my lack of formal education in journalism, my determination to learn and improve on a daily basis while also taking chances for great opportunities helped me get to where I am. Experiences such as becoming an editor at the FanSided network, a contributor for Yahoo! Sports, and a Featured Columnist with Bleacher Report prepared me for my full-time role on the numberFire content team and shaping me into the sportswriter I am today.

Are you a passionate sports fan with a desire to share your opinion with other like-minded individuals? Are you looking for a fun way to generate a second income? Do you want to make a complete career change? How about a combination of those options? Well, you can get there.

Everyone deserves to do something they're passionate about. No matter how unattainable it appears, don't listen to naysayers. The goal living inside you was placed there for a reason. With enough hard work and willingness to continuously learn, it will be reached.

When some people jump right in without a plan, getting the ball rolling can be difficult. In fact, it's so difficult that they quit before seeing the fruit of their labor.

Clearly defining attainable goals, having the confidence to get started, and not overloading yourself at the beginning is more than half the battle. I'm here to help you faithfully make this jump with a plan in place.

CHAPTER 1:

What Should You Write About?

Finding your niche sounds like a complicated process that takes hours, days, or even weeks of soul searching to figure out. Not so much. It boils down to one simple question: what do you love talking about the most?

Instead of a long and drawn out process, finding your niche can be as easy as three quick steps. Ready to find out what you should be writing about and what will be most enjoyable?

This should probably take less than 10 minutes. I know we do everything on our phones and computers these days but grab a blank sheet of paper and a pen. Something about physically touching it just sounds better to me.

Now, let's get down to business:

Step 1: List all the sports and teams you love and follow (from most to least).
Step 2: Write down the websites you frequent to consume content about these sports/teams.
Step 3: In a few words, explain why these sites are your "go-to" for sports information.

Instead of just thinking about favorite teams, sports, and websites, you can now actually see what you love and why you love it.

Whatever tops the list is likely what you're most "qualified" to write about, while the websites you regularly visit shine light on your potential writing style (funny, serious, analytical, etc.).

See? That wasn't so painful.

Before officially proclaiming your niche, ensure all options are considered. There are endless topics to focus on as a sportswriter, but niches normally fall into three different categories: single-sport, multi-sport, or a single topic within a sport(s).

When first starting out, it's important to have a focused niche. Many people are passionate about multiple teams or sports and want to dedicate a blog to everything they love.

There's nothing wrong with that, but keep in mind how much work it is. One of the keys to be a successful sportswriter is not spreading yourself too thin—especially at the beginning.

It's easy to say you want to have a New York sports blog based on the Mets, Giants, Knicks, and Rangers because you're a passionate fan of all four teams, but there's also no offseason. Given the 24-hour news cycle, there will be plenty of overlap, regardless of which teams are in season.

Having no offseason isn't a big deal at first because you're all jacked up about putting thoughts and opinions on virtual paper for the whole world to see. However, being a writer can be a grind, and not burning out too quickly is vital toward overall success and longevity.

Instead of going for everything all at once, make it a gradual progression. Maybe start with just the Mets and Giants, then eventually add in the Knicks and Rangers as things continue going in the right direction.

A great example of someone picking a niche and sticking with it is Tim Dierkes. He's the man behind MLB Trade Rumors, Hoops Rumors, Pro Football Rumors, and Pro Hockey Rumors.

When Tim first started his sportswriting career, he was most passionate about baseball, specifically all the hot stove news that happens during the offseason. With that in mind, he started a site solely dedicated to baseball news, rumors, and trades.

Putting it simply, Dierkes created a site with a single-sport niche: Major League Baseball.

If you're a baseball fan, chances are you've spent quite a bit of time on MLBTR. As the site grew, became a legitimate news source, and was staffed with more writers, readers consistently asked Dierkes to expand this service to other sports.

Although MLBTR was very successful, it took him years before doing the same thing for another sport. Eventually, Hoops Rumors was established, which had the same goal, but dedicated to the NBA.

Putting it simply again, the addition of Hoops Rumors meant Dierkes expanded to a multi-sport niche.

Almost immediately, it seemed as if readers wanted him to continue expanding beyond the NBA and MLB. His next move didn't happen quickly, but Pro Football Rumors appeared to cover every rumor and piece of news in the NFL before doing the same for the NHL with Pro Hockey Rumors.

For anyone wanting to start a website and make it "big," Dierkes is the example to follow with regard to choosing a niche: start small and focus on being great, then expand when the time is right.

As the old saying goes, "It's better to be great at one thing, instead of just OK at a lot of things."

That couldn't ring truer in this case. Before expanding his business, it was important for each site to reach a certain point.

Finalizing a niche is completely up to you. After all, you'll be the one writing, so you must be happy with it. Going for the grand slam right at the beginning is easy, but there's a high risk of burnout and failure. Focusing on one particular sport or team will make life easier in a multitude of ways.

You're only one person with a limited amount of time. Consistency—which we'll talk about soon—is important, but quality over quantity is key toward building a dedicated and engaged following.

Now that you've figured out what you'll be writing about, the next phase in this process is pretty important. Why? Because you need to have a site to publish all these unique opinions!

Creating and Designing Your Blog

Should creating and designing a blog be a long, complicated, and sometimes expensive process? It can be, but it all depends on the amount of work put in.

If you're looking for a site that's professionally done and you have no background in doing such a thing, you'll be outsourcing these duties to someone who can. If you'd rather learn on the fly and personally get deep into the project, it's actually a lot of fun. This allows you to feel more invested and have a greater sense of pride since it was "built with your own two hands."

Nowadays, creating a blog with a personalized URL takes seconds. While there are numerous blog platforms to choose from, Wordpress is by far the easiest and most user-friendly to navigate, speaking from my experience.

Many people would rather not throw a bunch of money into a blog until feeling more comfortable, and there's nothing wrong with that. If that's the case, wordpress.com is the place to start. In order to own a site, you must do the following:

Step 1: Log on to **wordpress.com**.
Step 2: Sign up for an account.
Step 3: Identify what to name your blog and what it will be about, along with stating the primary goal.
Step 4: Select a URL name.
Step 5: Pick a WordPress plan that makes sense for you.

And just like that, you're a blog owner. It's really that easy. It probably won't take long to notice there's a wordpress.org in addition to wordpress.com. They're from the same company, so what could be different?

Setting up on WP.org takes a bit longer, but there are blog plugin options available in the dashboard for site enhancements, among other things. There are clear advantages to WP.org over WP.com, but that doesn't mean people not ready for WP.org must start there. Getting into the groove of writing consistently is more important than anything else. Switching your blog from one platform to another is common, and WordPress has services to facilitate the process.

While I recommend starting a blog via WordPress because that's what worked best for me, there are tons of different content management systems to choose from depending on personal preferences and writing style. Some include (not all are free):

- Blogger
- Tumblr
- Sportsblog.com
- Typepad
- Medium
- RebelMouse

Once a blog is finally in place, configuring the optimal background and sidebar widgets to display on the homepage is entirely up to you.

There are two things every blog must have: an "About me" page and a "Contact me" page.

When someone stumbles upon your work and becomes intrigued, they'll want to learn more about you. Don't force them to go anywhere else for that information. Keep them engaged right on your site.

Sometimes, people will be so intrigued by your writing that they'd like to personally reach out with a message instead of leaving a comment. Again, provide this opportunity directly on your site. Plus, it's a good place to display social media links or buttons.

Having complete control over designing a site—especially when you've never done anything like it before—is intimidating. However, there is no better way to take ownership of this new venture and learn all aspects of having a blog.

The more time you spend taking care of non-writing details to improve your site, the more invested and prouder you'll feel while spreading the word.

Nervous about the site not looking perfect on the first try? Well, throw that notion out the window. On The Way Home went through at least four or five different designs (I honestly lost count) before I was satisfied. The beauty of owning your own blog is having the flexibility to try something without experiencing any barriers (i.e. making requests to a design team).

You may love the design on Monday but end up hating it by Friday and completely change it. And you know what? That's OK! It's your site; you can do whatever you want.

This may not be part of the journey you were expecting to deal with but embrace it. You're unique. Readers will see this through the articles produced, along with getting a glimpse of your personality with how the site is designed.

CHAPTER 2:

The Importance of a Content Strategy

Regardless of your writer identity, creating a content strategy is vital toward eventually experiencing success.

Having a plan makes execution much easier, allowing you to focus on quality. Sitting down with article ideas already in hand takes the guesswork out, which leaves creating top-notch content the only thing to be concerned with. Many sports blogs focus on breaking news and trending stories. Paying attention to niche-specific current events is something all sites should do, but don't be concerned with pumping out articles for every single rumor or piece of news.

If you catch a story before it gets big, the sharing potential through various social media outlets is huge—especially if the URL gets into the right hands. However, there are already thousands of websites and blogs with larger audiences doing this effectively. In order to retain new readers, giving them a legitimate reason to come back by producing unique content is key. Getting them in the door is great but keeping them in the building must be the long-term goal.

How is this done correctly? By sharing your opinion fearlessly, while also writing headlines appealing to both humans and search engines.

Fans see the same news articles or trending stories hundreds of times. Using current events as the basis of an original article is a better usage of your time and has greater potential to catch a reader's eye.

Some of the most shareable articles are lists. The longer it is, the better, but if you can't do that, odd-numbered lists also perform very well. Let's say your niche is the New York Mets and it's the offseason. Some clickable headlines that would attract diehard fans and new readers include:

"7 Trades the New York Mets Should Make This Winter"
"9 Ways to Fix the New York Mets in 2016"
"10 Free Agents the New York Mets Should Consider"
"The 20 Greatest Moments in New York Mets History"

While effective, lists are also exhausting and time-consuming. Plus, your blog needs some diversity—it can't be solely comprised of lists. This is where your opinion comes into play. Some examples of editorial headlines include:

"Why The 2016 New York Mets *Will* Make the Playoffs"
"*How* to make the New York Mets a Playoff Contender in 2016"
"*Why* David Wright is Vital towards the New York Mets' Success"
"The New York Mets *Should* Pursue (insert name)"

The most important words in the above headlines (outside of the keywords) are in italics. Saying "why," "how" and "should" implies there's a specific slant.

Just as a reader may agree with your take on a free-agent signing or trade, there will be others who disagree. As much as we'd like to think it's possible, we can't and won't please everyone. There are millions of passionate sports fans out there. Whether they like what you say or not, if an article you write gets them talking, debating and/or sharing with others, it's a success. Don't lose sight of that.

You'll likely be the sole contributor in the beginning stages of your blog, so being consistent with content is crucial. This shows readers they can count on reading unique articles regularly, and more article URLs available means more opportunities for search engines to capture your work.

Also, more articles published equals more concrete opportunities to promote your blog, even when you're not physically doing it.

A majority of content consumption is done during the week (Monday through Friday), meaning these are the best days to publish articles. Learning to take a break—whether it's on the weekend or another time—is important for a couple reasons. Not only does it prevent burnout, but it also allows for time to plan.

If two or more articles can be published per day, that's fantastic. Time is almost always of the essence, though, so posting once a day is acceptable. The time of year will dictate subject matter, but that shouldn't stop you from having an idea of how to approach each day.

When I started On the Way Home, my ever-changing work schedule made having a content strategy a necessity. Here's how I structured it:

Monday: Series of the week — picking one head-to-head matchup and breaking down why each game was a must-watch.
Tuesday: MLB Diamond Notes — Taking four or five big stories from the past week and giving an opinion in a mailbag style.
Wednesday: This Day in Baseball History — Taking a look back at some monumental moments in baseball (including big games, birthdays of legendary

players, etc.).
- **Thursday**: A look at "Unbreakable" Records — Breaking down whether a current record (career hits, home runs, etc.) would ever be broken and who currently had the best chance.
- **Friday**: MLB Hall of Fame series — Going back to the inaugural HOF class and talking about each year's inductees week-by-week.

As you can see, three of five days dealt with MLB history. That gave me the opportunity to write whenever time permitted throughout the week, completing them ahead of schedule. Usually, the framework and idea for each topic regarding history was virtually finished in one evening.

Since my blog included past, present, and future topics, there had to be a proper mix. While getting my feet wet in sportswriting, emphasizing the past gave me a chance to write when I was feeling especially creative and had time.

This content plan also included different kinds of articles to keep readers stimulated. Mondays, Wednesdays, and Thursdays were more persuasive and opinionated. Tuesdays and Fridays were essentially lists.

Honestly, nobody knows how you work better than yourself. Forming a content strategy should be a personal endeavor, tailored to your schedule and habits. The beginning stages of a writing career is all about building confidence and setting yourself up best for success.

Having a plan in place is comforting to some, but others may feel more stress from it. It's all about personal preference. However, having at least some predetermined thoughts with regard to article styles and ideas does help content production become an easier task.

Forming and executing a plan of attack—either written in stone or something more fluid—is important toward giving your blog an identity and showing readers a general idea of what unique content to anticipate on a regular basis.

You want to stand out from the crowd, not blend in. With the right amount of preparation, you can focus on producing original and engaging content others will notice.

Staying Consistent With Grammar

Being a sportswriter is unique from being a "regular" writer because you must also be familiar with different lingo and sport-specific phrases. While being grammatically sound is preferred, following the same principles throughout an article is key.

It's frustrating to watch somebody neglect writing out cardinal and ordinal numbers under 10 at the beginning of an article, only to switch later on. Or, people using "homerun" and "home run" in the same piece.

Bleacher Report used to be the best with providing the necessary tools to have impeccable grammar. However, their custom style guide is no longer available for everyone to see – they've locked it up and have thrown away the key.

All blogs and websites have a different set of rules for grammar and language. So, this is the perfect opportunity to get familiar with niche-specific words and phrases, along with learning to stay consistent.

If you Google "Bleacher Report Style Guide", you'll still see the basics -- numbers and statistics (zero through nine, 10 or more and percentages), punctuation (quotation marks, unspaced em-dashes and serial commas), along with formatting and layout (headlines, paragraphs and quotations).

These areas are a lot to absorb in one sitting, but it's a good start. Becoming consistent takes focus, especially if you have some bad habits. Doing this now makes adjusting to bigger and more established websites as a contributor easier once that time comes.

Although the "Style Standard Clearinghouse" and "Sports Usage Dictionary" are no longer available to the public, there are other options to investigate. I'd suggest just looking at some of your favorite websites and see how they style certain terms and phrases specific to your niche.

Don't feel the need to memorize, though. Abiding by what you see strictly from memory takes away from the creative process. Fixing those bad habits and inconsistencies can take place in the editing phase, not the first draft.

Certain terms and phrases are displayed differently depending on the sport. Some people are vain enough that they'll dismiss the legitimacy of a writer's work if they don't know "home run" is two words and not one.

Depending on your niche, creating a list of words and phrases most relevant to you in a separate document is helpful. The more you use this lingo properly, the sooner it'll become second nature. Read over the list once or twice a day (this should take no longer than five or 10 minutes). Getting increasingly familiar with them will eventually shave time off the editing phase.

Having impeccable grammar is the goal, but nobody is perfect, no matter how hard they try. It'd be easier to get everything right the first time, but again, it's all a process. As you get more articles under your belt, those bad habits will start disappearing.

The editing phase seems like a waste of time, but it's essential toward publishing top-notch content.

Which is why you must….

Proofread, Proofread, and Proofread

This can't be stressed enough. The biggest mistake I made at the start of my sportswriting career—and one I'm still awfully embarrassed about—was never proofreading my work.

I know…awful!

I'm not sure what made me think this was OK, but it happened. Now, I'll never publish an article without proofreading it at least once or twice ever again.

Every writer has bad habits. Being too wordy is one of mine. After proofreading articles, I sometimes cut off as much as 100-200 words, which drastically improves the overall flow.

If I'm alone while composing an article, I'll read it aloud to make it easier to hear when something doesn't sound right. Again, nobody knows you better than you. Whatever is needed to polish up an article before hitting the publish button, make sure you do it.

Always strive for perfection, even though it doesn't always happen. Regardless of how much time is spent editing and proofreading, typos are unavoidable. Don't be discouraged about missing them because nobody is perfect but be sure to learn from them.

CHAPTER 3:

Establishing a Social Media Presence

There are countless social media services available. Due to how life is these days, you likely already have a presence on a few, but which one is most important for a successful sportswriting career?

While watching news-reporting shows on channels like ESPN, MLB Network, NFL Network and many others, insiders are breaking news in one place, and it's rarely on Facebook or Instagram.

It's almost always on Twitter.

Having a consistent presence on multiple platforms is great—especially because of the potential audience and overall reach—but your emphasis should be on creating and growing a dedicated Twitter following.

Not on Twitter yet? That's OK but sign up immediately. This is the best place to find influencers in your niche and study what they're doing to attract followers. Getting set up takes a few minutes, and all you need is the following:

Full name
Email address
A password
Professional-sounding username

Once that's done, click on the "sign up" button, and you're on Twitter!

How to Create a Following on Twitter

The beauty of Twitter is you can literally find people talking about any topic imaginable at any time of day. There is always a reachable audience on this space for all niches—big or small.

Before interacting with people in your niche, focus on making your profile pristine and legit. Don't worry; it doesn't take much longer than signing up for the service itself.

Here's an easy step-by-step checklist of what to complete before starting to branch out:

Deciding on an appropriate Twitter handle

Deciding on a Twitter handle comes down to personal preference, but there are a few things to consider. At this point in your writing career, only your blog exists. Some writers like using their blog's name as a username, yet others use their own name (I'm @mmusico8).

There are benefits to both. Having a matching blog name and Twitter handle is good for branding purposes, but long-term goals must also be considered. Are you planning to build this blog into a moneymaking site? If so, then heavily consider this option.

On the other hand, is this blog in existence to provide enough writing experience to propel you into being a well-known personality/featured contributor on a bigger platform? If so, then using your name should be heavily considered.

Whichever route you choose, making it professional is most important. Nobody should be cringing when a peer shares your Twitter handle.

Uploading the right profile picture and background

To be viewed as a legitimate profile (i.e. not spam), you must have a profile picture. Similar to choosing a Twitter handle, it should be professional, and preferably a headshot. If multiple social media services are used for sportswriting purposes, try using the same picture everywhere for consistency.

Associating your background with something niche-specific also makes a lot of sense. Since this is already something you're passionate about, it also gives followers a look into your personality.

Crafting a bio specifically for your target audience

As I said before, Twitter is great because you can find just about anyone talking about anything…as long as proper hashtags and words are used.

Those active on social media are likely already aware of niche-specific hashtags. Within the Mets Twittersphere, hashtags like #Mets, #LGM and #MetsTwitter are used hundreds and thousands of times on a daily basis.

A good bio tells potential followers who you are and what you do, while also making yourself searchable. When this is complete, it's time to venture out and start building credibility with others your niche.

It takes time to build a large and interactive following, but here are some simple, yet effective tips to get your work in front of more people on Twitter.

1. Start following people in your niche! Following influencers is a must, but also take a look at who is following the influencers. After all, they're the ones most likely to start reading your content more than anyone else.
2. Share your own content, but don't be afraid to share content from others. Writing a short comment, followed by the link and tagging the author is a great way to network without meeting face-to-face. Plus, they're more apt to follow you back, check out your stuff and share it occasionally with their larger following.
3. Be consistent. If someone clicks the follow button on your page, don't disappoint! If you're not sharing content, be sure to provide opinions and short analysis on current events—with the appropriate hashtags—so those searching can discover you. It'll make you appear more human to followers, while also building your reputation within the niche.
4. Advertise your Twitter handle (and other social media pages) everywhere. On your website, at the end of every article in a tagline, in your email signature, and anywhere else possible.
5. Make sure you're consistently following people and interacting with them. Your presence on Twitter isn't just going to magically grow—it's going to take effort. Following 20-30 people within your niche each week and starting conversations with them are great ways to start building relationships, along with credibility.
6. For those people who "randomly" follow you, interact with them! Reach out to say thank you and start a conversation. Getting followers is crucial but holding onto them is overlooked too often.

Knowing the Best Times to Tweet

Again, people are following you because you share quality content—both yours and from others—so you can't let those followers down.

What's the main reason why all sportswriters are on Twitter?

To be seen.

Every time a tweet is sent, we secretly hope people see it and are inspired enough to share. No sportswriter hopes their opinions and thoughts aren't seen. If that's the case, they're probably in the wrong industry.

Finding the peak times to post on Twitter is something everyone would like to know. While there have been studies done with regard to which days and times are generally better, it's unique to each user. How could we possibly find out these crucial details?

Thankfully, there is a fantastic service called **Tweriod** that does the heavy lifting. It's as simple as heading to the website and logging in with your Twitter account. This gives them access to your followers to analyze their activity.

Within a couple hours, you'll receive an email stating a personalized report is ready to view. This report displays the details of when your followers are active on Twitter throughout each day of the week.

The best part for a novice sportswriter not looking to break the bank is it's absolutely free.

After reviewing each facet of the report, I strongly recommend syncing Tweriod with **Buffer**, which is a social media scheduling tool. Instead of guessing when the best peak time is, Buffer does it for you. All you need to do is compose a tweet, add it to the queue and it will automatically be sent at the next peak time.

There are tons of Twitter tools out there, but these two specifically took my account to the next level. I joined Twitter in the summer of 2010 but didn't start tweeting consistently for sportswriting purposes until August 2011.

From that moment through July 2014, my following had reached about 700 people. Not huge, but it was a solid base to be seen, appear credible and get decent referral traffic. Upon discovering Tweriod and Buffer, the wealth of free information I received focused my social sharing around the most important times.

My four peak times on Twitter each day were: 7:32am, 2:29pm, 5:25pm and 8:09pm (all EST). By tweeting the same amount I always had (maybe even less), my following grew to over 1,100 within the following six months.

Tweriod and Buffer provide the knowledge and tools necessary to make being seen and getting articles shared a reality without forking over a penny.

Don't stop tweeting at non-peak times altogether—especially since you'll be interacting with others on a regular basis. When it comes to sharing content, though, use these peak times as a guide on a day-to-day basis.

Properly Utilizing Other Social Media Networks

You understand why I think Twitter is the most important social media network. But is it the only one you should have a presence on? Absolutely not!

With regard to joining multiple networks, it's much better to have a great presence on a few instead of an "eh" presence on a lot. Remember – quality almost always outweighs quantity.

Whether you're on a social media network for fun or for business, always think about how to leverage it to provide value for your blog and continue building a brand.

Organic reach on Facebook is not nearly as good as it used to be, and it's not getting better anytime soon. Many people tend to think having a Facebook page dedicated to a blog is not worth the time, but it is.

No matter how awful organic reach is, Facebook is still the most popular social media network out there. It's also worth noting that logging on is the first thing many people do upon waking up.

There are plenty of opportunities to strategically gain new readers. Once the time comes and you're comfortable spending some money, promoting your page or a popular article can increase your audience more than you'd ever imagine. And it could happen with as little as $50.

Another popular social media network sports blogs and websites are active on is Instagram. It's basically Facebook with pictures, but with much better organic reach. It makes plenty of sense to be active on this platform, as well.

Plus, if you enjoy doctoring photos or have a friend that enjoys such a thing, it's a great way to stand out. The only difference between Instagram and most other networks is they don't allow live links in posts. However, they do allow a link in profile bios, which sites use to leverage special articles.

Knowing When to Recycle Old Content

New content is constantly being created, along with sharing the work of other networked connections. In the world of sports, many articles grow stale reasonably quickly due to the news cycle and whether a sport is in season or not.

If the team you cover makes a big free agent signing and you write about it, that article likely won't be relevant in a couple of months. However, the ones looking back on historic moments (among others) are considered evergreen content.

So, no matter how much time goes by, the article remains relevant in some way.

Use this to your advantage. Properly repurposing articles allows you to continue reaping the benefits of your hard work long after the publish button was initially pushed.

If you put together an article recounting the top 20 moments in Mets history in November, don't let anyone stop you from sporadically repurposing it at least throughout the remainder of the offseason.

This doesn't just apply to evergreen content, either. Let's use the Mets signing David Wright to a contract extension as an example.

Once this news broke, you put together a killer article detailing why this was the right (or wrong) move for New York and what kind of production they should expect over the life of this deal. Once published, you tweeted it out at one of those pre-determined peak times.

It got some traction, but you hoped for more. Don't hesitate to tweet it out again later on while it's still applicable. Posting at peak times allows maximum exposure to followers. However, doing it at a different peak time lends the possibility of others who haven't seen it before to potentially share the link hours, days, or sometimes weeks after getting published.

That's why plenty of sportswriters use the "ICYMI" acronym when repurposing content. It's a subtle way of saying, "Yea, I already tweeted this, but wanted to do it again in case other people didn't see it yet."

Leveraging Twitter for your sportswriting career is intimidating because there are so many people out there, but that's also the beauty of it. On any given day and at any given time, there is an audience waiting to listen and interact with you.

Taking things one step at a time is crucial. Before letting yourself loose on Twitter—or any other network—be sure you've accomplished what we already talked about. Here's another quick checklist:

1. Your profile looks professional.
2. Stay consistent with a social media strategy.
3. Continually share your content and content from others.
4. Follow niche-specific influencers, along with their followers, and interact with

    them to start forming relationships.
5. Always use appropriate hashtags to ensure maximum exposure to like-minded individuals.

As long as these five things are kept in mind, your following on Twitter and any other social media network will consistently increase and be an asset instead of a hindrance.

Here's a Secret to Boost Your Twitter Following

You're doing everything we talked about on Twitter, but it's taking forever to see results. Let me be the first to tell you this is absolutely normal, so there's no point in being worried.

Whether your following is big or small, what's most important is how engaged they are.

If you type "how to get more Twitter followers" into the old Google machine, you'll see tons of services offering hundreds and even thousands of followers for what seems like a cheap price. Don't do it. Most of the time, they'll just pump up your following with a bunch of fake profiles. And, fake profiles mean a less engaging crowd.

One service that doesn't do this is a company called **Social Quant**. As you can see from their website, they boast growing your following and engagement drastically in a short amount of time.

What this service does is ask you to provide up to 20 keywords associated with whom you'd like to connect, allowing them to go out and find them by following and unfollowing on your behalf. If people they follow don't follow back, they will eventually unfollow.

There is a paid service available, but they also offer a two-week free trial before having to commit to anything. So, if you feel as though you've reached a plateau on Twitter and could use a little boost, I'd suggest doing the two-week trial. I did this and felt as though the service connected me with a bunch of people relevant to my niche. Plus, they were all real people, which is what's most important.

CHAPTER 4:

Taking Your Blog to the Next Level

The honeymoon period is officially over—the blog has been in existence for a few months, you feel comfortable sharing your opinion publicly ,and a dedicated following has appeared. Page traffic numbers are trending in the right direction, but they could always be better.

The time has finally come to take your blog to the next level. Here are a few options to make this a reality.

Applying to join a larger network of blogs

There are networks like **SportsBlog** and **The Sports Daily** with large audiences that exist specifically to be a platform for other independent blogs to be seen more than ever before. Not only do they help a site's credibility, but the increased amount of quality inbound links headed your way also improves SEO rankings.

It's very simple to inquire if your blog meets the network's standards. An example of the benefits detailed on The Sports Daily's site include some of the following:

1. A professionally designed website that's customized to fit your needs.
2. Design of custom banners and graphics to help brand the blog.
3. Help with advertising, hosting and blogging best practices.
4. Editorial freedom (which should never be overlooked).
5. Your content promoted through widgets, portals and syndication agreements.
6. A solid community to collaborate with others.

The best part of all is your blog is a part of this network, but still independent. That means you maintain 100 percent control of the site, the content published and how day-to-day operations are handled.

Getting referral traffic from Sports Reference, LLC

As an avid sports fan, you've probably checked out a player's online stats page more than a few times. Depending on your niche, there's a familiarity with certain sites more than others.

One group of sites most—if not all—sports fans are familiar with include those in the Sports Reference, LLC family (Baseball-Reference, Hockey-Reference, Pro-

Football-Reference and Basketball-Reference). You can use these sites to help boost referral traffic on your blog.

Again, let's use David Wright as an example. If you go to his Baseball-Reference page, you'll see a spot for "Player News" along with his actual statistics. These are blogs utilizing the site's player linker feature. This is a great way to receive more inbound links and get tremendous amounts of referral traffic.

The article doesn't even have to be focused on David Wright—as long as you mention a player's first and last name while properly using the linker, your article will appear on their page.

Don't miss out on a huge opportunity like this. Click on the "Add Your Blog Posts Here" link and read through the simple application process to be included on the stats page of any player you ever mention going forward.

Posting articles to all valid social media profiles

Sharing content consistently on Twitter has been mentioned repeatedly, but don't forget about those other social media networks. While there are automation services available—such as TwitterFeed—I've found it's best to share posts manually, especially if only one or two are being published per day.

The biggest downside to using TwitterFeed is the formatting of automated posts remains the same across all platforms. Since each network is unique to one another, the formatting of a successful post will be different on Twitter, Facebook, Google+ and so on.

It will take a few extra minutes, but figuring out how to format a post and market it correctly on each social media network is just as effective as knowing your personal peak times to post. Again, remember that it's quality you should be concerned about, not quantity.

Is saving time important at the start of your sportswriting career? I've already said it is, especially when you likely make your living during the 9am to 5pm hours. However, whether you're ramping up your blog to the next level or looking for ways to improve the promotion of content, automating social media posts should be a last resort.

Networking with others in your niche

Networking with others and forming niche-specific relationships is an ongoing practice. This is one of those times when it comes in handy.

Upon first breaking into sportswriting, it's tough to immediately ask connections for favors—mostly because you don't have a reputation within the industry or a real relationship with anyone yet.

Once your blog is established and you begin looking more credible, that changes. Reach out to contacts and offer things such as:

1. **Guest posting opportunities (on their site and yours).** This gets your work in front of different readers, while also providing the opportunity to link back to your blog. Getting others to post on your blog is an easy way to publish more original content without actually writing more.
2. **Content and link-swapping partnerships.** This allows both sites involved to get valuable inbound links directed back to one another. Again, this builds up your site with more content in a much easier way.
3. **Utilizing link submission opportunities.** Sites like MLB Trade Rumors allow smaller sites to submit articles with the possibility of getting linked in a weekly feature. What you get in return is tremendous exposure and referral traffic, along with another quality inbound link.
4. **Submitting articles to social bookmarking sites.** There are a lot in existence, but the best one is Reddit because there is what feels like a million sub-reddits that drill down to super specific niches. These are best for any lists and potentially viral content.

All these tactics have one thing in common: getting links pointing back to your site. The more it's accomplished, the better your SEO ranking will eventually be, moving articles higher in search results. A lot of hard work is involved but staying consistent will lead to seeing a difference.

Sending tips on little-known stories to larger sites

Larger sites like Bleacher Report, SB Nation, and Deadspin have enough staff writers to produce both trending stories and original content continuously. However, they don't always see potentially viral stories as quickly as others.

With all your networking, getting an early scoop on a story or stumbling upon a little-known video that will eventually get a lot of publicity will be more possible than you think.

After publishing a story on your site and posting to social media, send it to these larger sites via the tips email addresses advertised. If deemed legit, they'll publish an article and give you credit by linking and/or mentioning you. Since these sites have the best reach and reputation in the industry, you'll reap huge dividends with regard to referral traffic, along with getting another high-quality inbound link.

Join writer associations

Depending on what your niche is, there are writer associations out there to join. Doing so will not only help you continue networking with other like-minded people within the industry, but also provide the opportunity for more blog exposure in the form of tweets and inbound links.

I've been a member of two associations affiliated with baseball writers: the IBWAA (the Internet Baseball Writers Association of America) and the BBBA (Baseball Bloggers Alliance).

Being a part of the IBWAA allows me to be a part of a group that has its own votes on things like end-of-season awards and the Baseball Hall of Fame, which is pretty fun. With the BBBA, it was all about being a part of an organization dedicated to getting the word out about independent blogs.

There are certain requirements to join, but they're generally very attainable. If baseball is not your niche, go ahead and search for others to join and see what the requirements are. There is the PFWA (Pro Football Writers of America), the FSWA (Fantasy Sports Writers of America), the PBWA (Pro Basketball Writers of America) and plenty more – it's just a matter of finding out what exists.

Practicing What I Preach

Talking about all this stuff is great, but does it really work right now? The experiences I went through with On The Way Home were valuable in helping move my writing career forward, but that blog hasn't been active since 2013. Lots of stuff can happen between then and now.

I'm not sure if it was the excitement of the Winter Meetings or something else, but I decided to start a new baseball blog on my own in the beginning of December 2015, called Chin Music. Since my work schedule was pretty hectic, the focus of this blog at the start was to provide editorial commentary and opinionated articles about Major League Baseball no less than twice a week.

Without posting articles on a daily basis, I had to focus even more on quality and getting people talking.

To help get the word out, I used the tips I've outlined earlier in this book. As I began building up the number of written articles, the two techniques I used included the Baseball-Reference linker and submitting articles each week to MLB Trade Rumors for the Baseball Blogs Weigh In feature.

From the beginning of December to the end of January, I went from zero page views to more than 11,000. Considering the only other ways I advertised were through Facebook or Twitter, this was pretty encouraging.

Once I felt as though there was enough content available, I applied to join the Bloguin network (now known as The Sports Daily), which was accepted. They helped build me an entirely new site, just like they said. So, I went from a very minimalist and simple design on my own WordPress site to a much more professional-looking and branded site.

The results may not happen that quickly for you, but I wanted to give you an idea of how it can work. I'm not just saying that doing these things would be a good idea – I do them myself.

CHAPTER 5:

Taking Your Credibility to the Next Level

Whether the goal is to make your blog profitable or to use it as a springboard to become a full-time writer elsewhere, branching out is important.

While each site is different, becoming a contributor isn't much of an extra burden in addition to your current writing schedule. Here are ways to make your resume look even more attractive to prospective employers.

Joining sites with superior reach as a staff writer or contributor

Creating original content as a contributor or staff writer for larger sites gets your work seen by more people than ever before. It also provides the opportunity to network and collaborate with other well-known writers.

When thinking about places to write for with superior reach, **Bleacher Report** is usually the first site mentioned. While this is a great resume builder, the application process had always very selective and opportunities have now become much less open.

SB Nation is similar to B/R, but different because they have dedicated team sites with a staff led by editors with a specific vision. Being a staff writer means there are weekly and/or monthly quotas attached to article creation.

FanSided is similar in scope to SB Nation because writers can join a dedicated site as a staff writer and are expected to produce original content on a consistent basis.

These sites are all selective, but B/R and SB Nation have historically been more selective than FanSided. With all the experience and connections you've accumulated at this point, earning a gig like one of these should be attainable.

Your resume is being built with each article produced for these kinds of sites, but it can also still benefit your personal blog. Using a tagline at the end of articles will advertise your Twitter handle and blog URL to the largest audience you've ever written for.

Taking advantage of continuing education opportunities

Since these sites have incredible reputations to uphold, they do everything possible to ensure those representing them have the necessary resources to be the best writers possible.

B/R and SB Nation both have style guides writers are expected to follow, maintaining consistency throughout the network. From personal experience with FanSided, it's not that strict with regard to style, but there was an internal blog specifically dedicated to content creation and how to be unique in an industry some may view as saturated. That was a little while ago, though, so times may have changed since then.

Applying for continuing education courses at B/R such as the Writer's Program and Bleacher Report University were great ways for me to get "formal" education. We never stop learning in this business and going through programs similar to these will continue honing skills while simultaneously adding bullets to your resume.

Taking the opportunity to be more than "just a writer"

You entered this industry for one reason: to write about sports. With the thought of branching out to diversify your resume, taking on different responsibilities in addition to "just writing" helps shine on other talents potential employers consider valuable.

Since networks like SB Nation and FanSided are large and contain over 300 dedicated sites each, they offer editor opportunities. It's a lot of work—especially for a side gig—but it's an experience you should try at least once if an interesting position becomes available.

If you do grab this kind of opportunity, throw those preconceived notions about being an editor out the window. It's much more than just proofreading and putting the finishing touches on articles from staff writers. Nowadays, an editor is expected to be the lead writer, social media manager and head talent recruiter, all while leading the content strategy and remotely managing (usually) unpaid staff writers.

Speaking from experience as a former editor for Rising Apple, it's an incredible amount of work. However, being truly passionate about the site's mission made it fun. Once positive results started flowing in, it was also rewarding.

Having experience as an editor is one of the things future employers want to see. This provides concrete evidence that your skills within sports journalism have multiplied, making you more attractive and versatile as a professional.

After experiencing what it's like to be an editor of a high-traffic site, one of two things will happen. Either you'll fall in love with the extra duties and responsibilities that come with it, or you'll realize you'd rather solely focus on creating quality and unique content as part of a group.

The great thing is that once you've served as an editor somewhere, nobody can take this resume builder away. The experience gained and credibility earned provides the opportunity to start turning this intense passion into a legitimate career.

CHAPTER 6:

Turning Your Passion into Profit

If you've read carefully throughout the previous chapters, your sportswriting career possesses everything necessary to have sustained success: writing experience, a dedicated social media following, connections within the industry and time as being more than "just a writer."

Taking the next step in this field depends on what those initial goals were.

Some enjoy the power of commanding a large online audience and are happy with writing on the side for fun. Others feel the same way, but also are interested in turning this passion into a profit. There's nothing wrong with getting compensated, especially when so much time is dedicated to it!

You're fully equipped to start getting paid, but it's sometimes hard finding the right fit. If the initial goal was to turn your personal blog into a moneymaking site, here are some options.

Featuring advertisements and sponsored posts

As mentioned before in joining a network like **The Sports Daily**, they provide independent blogs with advertisements to feature on their respective sites. Once earnings hit a certain threshold, members can cash in on a certain percentage of the revenue generated.

If your site brings in heavy traffic numbers on a monthly basis, this is an intriguing option to generate passive income, along with becoming an affiliate marketer.

Plenty of companies are willing to pay commission to others for generating referrals. Since your site has built up a large audience—both on the blog and via social media—all you must do is market this product or service to readers.

This works similarly to placing ads on your site. To find affiliate programs within your niche, sign up with **ClickBank** for free to apply to any featured members.

Upon getting accepted by the company you'd like to be affiliated with, they'll provide embed code(s) needed to display with a banner(s). These contain unique links to track every sale originating from the site it's placed on.

Depending on how engaged readers are, simply placing an ad on your site will generate revenue, but some work is needed to maximize it. There is usually no cap on earnings for affiliate marketers, so the more people you refer, the more money you make.

Finding a niche-specific product or service immediately provides a better chance at maximizing revenue. Other ways to generate as much money as possible through affiliate marketing include:

- Periodically writing posts advertising the product or service, with unique links included.
- Regularly posting the appropriate link on all valid social media channels.
- Posting in niche-specific forums online once you've participated enough and have proven to be more than a spammer.
- Sending out deals with appropriate links to email subscribers if you have a dedicated list (which you should).
- Including affiliate links in taglines at the bottom of relevant articles you write.

The best part about affiliate marketing is revenue can be generated around the clock—whether you're working or not. Since a good reputation has been built with past posts, readers will be landing on your site at all hours of the day on articles you've written weeks, months, and sometimes years ago.

Without actively plugging the company you're marketing for, they'll see the banner embedded in your site, and they could turn into a referral. Even though effort is needed to be successful, past effort never goes away.

And remember when we talked about the importance of getting quality inbound links from other sites for SEO purposes? Well, other companies are looking for just that in the form of sponsored posts, and there are some companies that are willing to pay bloggers a negotiated fee to have something published at your site.

Paid freelance writing opportunities

Branching out to become a contributor, staff writer, or editor at larger sites helps build resumes and credibility within the industry. If you find the right gig, they'll also pay you.

The best types of freelance writing jobs to land include those paying a flat fee per article written. These don't pop up often, but can be found by scouring websites like **Indeed**, **JournalismJobs.com**, **Craigslist**, the **ProBlogger Job Board** and various freelance sites like **odesk.com**, **guru.com** and **freelance.com**.

Beware, though. These sites have a lot of information and opportunities on them, so you'll have to carefully sift through for sports-related gigs.

Don't forget to try some quick Google searches, as well. The Internet is powerful.

The most common type of freelance gig available is correlated to an article's performance. Technically, this means your earning potential is unlimited because more page views equals more money. However, this makes all aspects of content creation and social media marketing very important.

Depending on positions available, **SB Nation** and **FanSided** also compensate writers. With all the added responsibilities given to editors, earning a share of advertising revenue your particular site generates each month is normally an incentive.

Most editors also double as lead writers, but there are ways to generate higher revenues without writing more often. Social media marketing of articles is crucial, but more content usually means more page views, leading to more impressions on ads. If you recruit a large and dedicated staff that adheres to article production quotas, you'll be writing just as much (or sometimes less) while the site is churning out more content overall.

As this happens and page views start piling up, your cut of the ad revenue increases. And that's good news.

If a freelance writing position is performance-based, a pay structure of $1 for every 1,000 page views generated (or something similar to that) is normal.

Again, a simple Google search will provide a number of options to investigate. **FanSided** has an incentive-based program in place, as do places like examiner.com, VAVEL.com, **numberFire** and **The Sports Daily.**

Due to the high demand for paid freelance jobs, many sites may not publicly advertise them unless someone inquires. Therefore, this is a great time to leverage specific connections made while finding the best opportunity.

When looking for the right gig, keep one thing in mind: never be afraid to ask. As Wayne Gretzky (and Michael Scott) said, "You miss 100 percent of the shots you don't take."

To apply to be considered, you'll usually be asked to provide a resume and writing sample. Some sites want an original article, but others simply want to see a link to previous work.

If they require an original sample, be bolder than normal to stand out.

When Bleacher Report had an open call for writers, applicants were required to submit original articles. After getting my first application rejected (I wrote about why the Chicago White Sox extending Chris Sale was a smart move), I knew I had to think outside the box.

So, I took a unique approach on the Mets' potential catching situation. At the time, Travis d'Arnaud was the starter, but minor leaguer Kevin Plawecki was anticipated to be ready for the big leagues sooner rather than later, which would've seemingly created logjam if neither were traded (man, have times changed).

I wrote an article arguing New York could employ a "two-headed monster" to keep their legs fresh throughout the regular season and ready for potential playoff games—similar to what NFL teams do with running backs.

Was it a coincidence that B/R accepted me after submitting this kind of article? Possibly, but I'm glad I took a chance by doing something different.

Finding full-time work

If the goal was to eventually make a complete career change and get into the sports journalism industry full-time when you started writing, congratulations! The steps you've taken and the time accrued in the field should have you well prepared to take on any future challenge.

The experience is there (writing, editing, social media management). Your resume is diversified with various skills, along with time at well-established sites. Most importantly, you've networked and formed relationships with other very connected people.

Honestly, you'll be successful at any job you land because the preparation is all done. The most daunting part will be the actual job search. There are lots of sportswriting opportunities, but even though some aren't high paying or glamorous, they're also in high demand.

An old adage heard in the business world is, "It's not what you know, but whom you know."

There's truth to that, but both are necessary to succeed. The "whom you know" part gets you in the door, but the "what you know" part keeps you in the building.

Putting yourself out there and being persistent will help you stand out from the crowd just as much as your writing skills do. When applying to jobs, always find someone to send an introductory email to after hitting the submit button. If you already have a relationship with a person who has connections within a particular company, don't be afraid to ask for help!

Simply reaching out to make a connection or asking for help can be the difference between getting a job interview and being overlooked. You've hustled yourself all the way to this point and it's fourth-and-goal at the one-yard line. Do what's necessary to punch the ball into the end zone—hand it off to Beast Mode instead of opting for a pass.

Thank You!

I hope you've enjoyed this book as much as I enjoyed writing it. Deciding to start a new career—whether it's on the side or full-time—is an exciting journey and I'm honored to be a part of yours.

As mentioned before, getting started is an overwhelming process given the industry's popularity. I applaud you for following your heart and immersing yourself in something you truly enjoy. It's a very rewarding feeling!

If you felt that this was helpful in getting your writing career off the ground, **please leave a review on Amazon** – I'd greatly appreciate it.

I also wanted to remind you of the other resources you can use on your sports blogging journey.

The contents of this book have been turned into an online course at Udemy. Retail price is $19.99, but all Sports Blogging 101 readers can use the SPORTSBLOGGING8 coupon code to access a 50% discount. I'd also love it if you joined my email newsletter by signing up at tinyletter.com/musicom.

Don't forget about the free 30-minute consultation I'm offering to help you get started. Send me an email at matt.musico8@gmail.com when you're ready.

I wish you the best of luck in your journey as a sportswriter! It will be a fun and rewarding experience to publish your own opinions about the teams and sports you love most. Once it's up and running, don't forget to share your site and Twitter handle with me so I can follow your work!

Made in the USA
San Bernardino, CA
12 December 2019